Dear Parents,

Welcome to the Magic School Bus!

For over 20 years, teachers, parents, and children have been enchanted and inspired by Ms. Frizzle and the fabulous cast of beloved characters that make up The Magic School Bus series.

The unusual field trips, visual jokes, eye-catching details, and interesting information are just a few of the elements that make The Magic School Bus series an excellent tool to get your child excited about school, reading, and exploring their world.

It is important that children learn to read well enough to succeed in school and beyond. Here are some ideas for reading this book with your child:

- Look at the book together. Encourage your child to read the title and make a prediction about the story.
- Read the book together. Encourage your child to sound out words when appropriate. When your child struggles, you can help by providing the word.
- Encourage your child to retell the story. This is a great way to check for comprehension.

Enjoy the experience of helping your child learn to read and love to read!

Visit www.scholastic.com/magicschoolbus to subscribe to Scholastic's free parent e-newsletter, and find book lists, read-aloud tips, and learning hints for pre-readers, beginners, and older kids, too. Inspire a love of books in your child!

There are many Magic School Bus books for your reader to enjoy. We think you will enjoy these, too:

Ms. Frizzle

Liz

Written by Kristin Earhart
Illustrated by Carolyn Bracken

Based on The Magic School Bus ® books
written by Joanna Cole and illustrated by Bruce Degen

The author and editor would like to thank Dr. Raymond J. Pupedis, Entomology Division, Yale-Peabody Museum of Natural History, New Haven, Connecticut, for his expert advice in preparing the manuscript and illustrations.

ISBN: 978-0-545-16727-7

12 11 10 9 8 7 6 5 4 3 2 1   10 11 12 13 14 15/0

Designed by Rick DeMonico

First printing, March 2010
Printed in the U.S.A.
40

The Magic School Bus® and the Butterfly Bunch

Arnold Ralphie Keesha Phoebe Carlos Tim Wanda Dorothy Ann

Cartwheel
·B·O·O·K·S·®

SCHOLASTIC INC.

New York Toronto London Auckland
Sydney Mexico City New Delhi Hong Kong

We get on the bus.
All at once, it starts to change.
Now it is a butterfly-bus.

9

The butterflies lay eggs.
When the eggs hatch,
they will be caterpillars.

All at once, the bus door opens.
We jump out.
Luckily, we have parachutes.

BABY BUTTERFLIES
by Wanda

Many insects grow in four stages.
When they are little, they do not
look like their parents.
Use this chart to follow a monarch
butterfly as it grows.

BUTTERFLY GROWTH CHART
1. egg
2. larva
3. pupa
4. adult
We are eggs now.

13

15

We keep eating.
We keep molting.
We keep growing.
Then we molt for the last time.
Now we have a hard shell.

EVERYTHING IS UPSIDE DOWN!

NO, ARNOLD. *WE'RE* UPSIDE DOWN.

We are cozy in our shells.
We go to sleep.
As we sleep, our bodies change.

ZZZZZZZ.

ZZZZZZZ.

ZZZZZZZ.

BUTTERFLY GROWTH CHART
1. egg
2. larva
3. pupa →
4. adult
Inside the shell, the caterpillar turns into a pupa, the third stage.

20

We go through our last change.
When we come out, we are butterflies.
Our wings are still wet.
We cannot fly.

CLASS, DRY YOUR WINGS BY FLAPPING.

THEN WHAT WILL HAPPEN?

WE'LL JUST WING IT.

"I'm hungry again," says Wanda.
"How do butterflies eat their food?"
Ralphie asks.
"They drink it!" the Friz answers.

The bird flies toward Arnold.
Arnold opens his wings.
And the bird flies away.

WHAT HAPPENED?

ARNOLD'S WINGS HAVE MARKINGS.

THEY LOOK LIKE EYES!

27

29

Back in the classroom, we draw pictures of our favorite butterflies.

31

MOTHS AND BUTTERFLIES

Butterflies and moths are related, yet there are several differences:

BUTTERFLIES

- Thin antennae with knobs at the end.
- Active during the day.
- Skinny bodies.
- Hold wings behind them at rest.
- Some are brightly colored.

MOTHS

- Thicker antennae, often feathery.
- Active at night.
- Plump, often hairy bodies.
- Open wings to sides when resting.
- Most are dull in color.

WHY DID THE CATERPILLAR CHEW A HOLE IN THE LEAF?

TO GET TO THE OTHER SIDE?

NO, BECAUSE IT WAS HUNGRY!